VIRTUAL
REAL ESTATE INVESTING
SECRETS

DC FAWCETT

Copyright © 2019 **DC FAWCETT**

All rights reserved. No part of this book may be reproduced, stored, or transmitted by any means—whether auditory, graphic, mechanical, or electronic—without written permission of both publisher and author, except in the case of brief excerpts used in critical articles and reviews. Unauthorized reproduction of any part of this work is illegal and is punishable by law.

www.virtualrealestateinvesting.club

TABLE OF CONTENTS

INTRODUCTION -- V

CHAPTER 1: Finding Virtual Markets -------------------------- 1

CHAPTER 2: Setting Up Your Virtual Business ---------------- 7

CHAPTER 3: Setting Up Social Media Systems -------------- 25

CHAPTER 4: Free Ways To Find Sellers ---------------------- 27

CHAPTER 5: Taking Calls From Sellers And Calling Sellers -- 45

CHAPTER 6: What's It Worth? ---------------------------------- 51

CHAPTER 7: Making Offers -------------------------------------- 57

CHAPTER 8: Overcoming The Top 5 Objections ------------ 65

CHAPTER 9: Getting The Contract Signed -------------------- 75

CHAPTER 10: Protecting Your Contract ------------------------ 77

CHAPTER 11: Free Ways To Find Buyers ---------------------- 83

CHAPTER 12: Qualifying Buyers --------------------------------- 95

CHAPTER 13: My Shortcut To Raising Money For Deals 101

CHAPTER 14: Setting The Price Of Your Deal --------------- 105

CHAPTER 15: Methods Of Closing Deals --------------------- 107

CHAPTER 16: Finding A Good Closing Agent ---------------- 113

CHAPTER 17: Managing The Deal Through Closing ------- 117

CHAPTER 18: Make More Money Per Deal ------------------ 119

CHAPTER 19: How To Do More Deals ------------------------ 131

CHAPTER 20: Automating Your Business -------------------- 135

CONCLUSION -- 139

INTRODUCTION

VIRTUAL REAL ESTATE INVESTING SECRETS is THE UNDERGROUND PLAYBOOK for Flipping Houses Anywhere in the World Without Leaving Your House.

This book will empower you to expand your business to new markets while outsourcing 100% of the work. You'll be able enter less competitive markets outside of your own local market so you can find and flip deals easier and faster.

You'll get the formula to find new markets where deals are easier to find and buyers are plentiful. You'll discover how to find and flip deals using simple social media strategies on Facebook and Youtube. You'll get the new way to make money in real estate without the capital restrictions associated with traditional real estate investing.

This Book Dispells the Big 3 Real Estate Myths. Have any of these false statements prevented you from moving forward in real estate?

1. I Need Big Money to Get Into Real Estate
2. I Need Good Credit to Make Money in Real Estate
3. I Need a Real Estate License to Get Into Real Estate

Virtual Real Estate Investing Secrets walks you through an alternative method to make money in real estate without using your own cash or credit and without spending months studying to get a real estate license. Read This Book as Soon as You Can and Discover the Secret to Financial Freedom.

You're Just 1 Deal Away...And it Can Happen Faster Than You Realize!

CHAPTER 1

FINDING VIRTUAL MARKETS

Let's discuss how to find virtual markets. So, there's a lot of online websites where you can find research on different types of real estate markets, what you want to look for is a viable market. A viable market is a market where you're able to wholesale deals that are available in the MLS.

Go to a site like Realtor.com, Zillow.com, or trulia.com where you get instant access to MLS properties and there are all different types of search criteria that you can search for. If you're searching for single-family homes with specific criteria and price points you can find it there, you can look at the price per square foot compared to the price and the square footage.

You also want to make sure that the area that you are working in the market that you're looking at working in has a population of at least a hundred thousand or more and it's not too rural.

A lot of times you can find great markets that are not the primary city of the state but they're secondary and third-tier markets in that area. And you want to make sure the area's average days on the market is 90 days or less because you want to make sure that when you find that market you're able to sell the property quickly.

The average days on market is that indicator that tells you if you can sell that property quickly or not.

The viable market criteria that I use for wholesale deals are prices that work to be able to flip them to landlords or rehabbers. For rehabbing, you want prices that work to be able to find virtual rehabbing partners that will be able to rehab those properties for you.

It's very similar to wholesaling to rehabbers because when you're wholesaling to a rehabber, you'll add your wholesale fee to the property. When you're rehabbing it yourself, you want to get a good deal as well so that you can buy it and build in your profit Margin.

And then, there are cash flow markets where you want to be able to buy properties that cash flow type properties for wealth building. You want a minimum of ten percent or greater cash on cash return preferably fifteen percent or greater cash on cash return.

Then, there's private lending... Private lending markets are markets where you can find experienced investors that will make your money work for you. They're going to do the work for you and you'll let your money work for you.

As a private lender, you lend money to rehabber, the rehabber does the work and pays you a high rate of return on your money. Your money is completely protected because it's secured by the property and if the rehabber defaults, you get the property.

I personally work with private lenders and if you are interested in becoming one of my private lenders, complete this form here.

Get a Free Report: *How to Become a Private Money Lender:* virtualrealestateinvesting.club/Lending

Let's go over how to find the best parts of town to target. The targeting criteria for specific zip codes is

For wholesaling to landlords, you want to look for the highest number of properties sold for cash sales that go to landlords. These are your rental neighborhoods where landlords are looking to buy the rental properties.

These are considered absentee owned sales that are financed with cash. These are typically the lowest average sale price for the area and identify the neighborhoods with the lowest priced homes and highest number of transactions.

I have a video tutorial of how you can do this in my FREE Mini-Course Bonus. Its Video #2 in this free series here: virtualrealestateinvesting.club/bonus

For wholesaling to rehabbers, you want to look for the highest number of cash sales at a higher price point with the lowest days on the market.

For rehab type properties you want to look at bread-and-butter type neighborhoods where people are owning the home to live in first-time homebuyers and greater. You do NOT want to have rental neighborhoods in these markets.

And for rehabbing, you want to look for the highest number of cash sales at a higher price point and the lowest days on the market. It's very similar to a wholesaling to rehabbers.

DC FAWCETT

CHAPTER 2

SETTING UP YOUR VIRTUAL BUSINESS

Many people kept on asking me, how I'm able to do so many deals all over the country without leaving my house. I was spending a lot of time teaching people one on one how I do my business which is why I decided to put all of my information in my processes and systems into this book.

My mission it to be able to touch a lot more lives and help a lot more people by teaching them virtual real estate investing. This book will show you step by step how to invest virtually all over the country from the comfort of your home.

I'm on a mission to change 10,000 lives over the next year and this book will give you the basics of virtual real estate investing. It's going to be able to change so many lives in the process. When you're ready to go deeper, you should consider getting my FREEDOM SYSTEM Home Study Course or join one of our Mentorship Programs.

And if you're reading this then you've committed to transforming your income and your life. I've written this book to solve two main issues facing new and seasoned real estate investors today.

The first issue is that a lot of investors can't seem to find good deals in their local market and so now with virtual real estate investing, you will no longer be handcuffed to your local market. You'll be able to invest and make money in virtual markets all over the country. There are tons of great markets right now that you could be working so this book will show you step-by-step how to do that.

You'll learn how to step out of your local market and invest virtually in growing and expanding markets flush with deals.

The second reason is, most people don't want to do all the work in the business and if you're anything like me you don't want to do all the work in your business.

You'd rather spend time doing things that you love to do like spending time with your family, fishing, boating, golfing or whatever you love to do.

This book is also going to show you how to outsource everything in the business, so you can run a virtual business not only in other markets of the country but also in your backyard as well without doing the work yourself. You don't need to go out in the field driving around and checking on your properties and meeting with sellers that don't show up to your appointments. You don't have to do that anymore because this book will show you how to get all that done for you.

And I'll show you how to outsource the entire process in your business in the upcoming chapters. The reason why we start our own business is to have true time freedom in our lives and if you're the one doing all the work in your business, then you've just created yourself a big job for yourself and I don't want you to get stuck in that trap. The purpose of the business is for the business to work for you not for you to work for the business and that's also what you'll learn throughout this book.

You need to think a little different, do things a little differently than the other programs and books you might have studied before and I'm going to show you how to do that. It's really not that difficult. You just need to know how to do it and you'll discover by simply copying what I do in my own business. I don't like to meet with sellers and I don't like to meet with buyers either. I think it's a waste of time for me to do that as the business owner. And so, I don't.

That's my choice and so my system is all designed around how to outsource all of those things effectively and you can do the same thing. If you don't want to meet sellers, you don't have to. If you don't want to meet buyers, you don't have to and I'm going to show you how to do all that.

I believe your business should fit you. You should not fit into a business model that you don't like or agree with, that's how I've designed the business because I've studied a lot of different programs and I've started a lot of different business models and a lot of them frankly, they just teach you how to get another job working for yourself. That doesn't make sense to me, I don't want to do that, I don't want to be handcuffed to the business.

I want to be able to take a month off and go here and there or not have to work when I don't want to. So, that's what this business and the system will show you. I wasn't personally happy with all the other real estate investing systems out there. So, I didn't want to do what they were telling me to do and this is why I'm sharing this with you, I believe that there are more people out there that are just like me because I prefer to do business from home on my terms when I want to.

I don't want to be wasting time running around town meeting with sellers and buyers that may or may not show up for a scheduled appointment, I'd rather spend that time doing things that I enjoy like spending time with my family. I mean isn't that what life is really about? It is for me.

Time is the most valuable asset that we have and it's the one resource we can never get back once it's spent. You can always get more money. It's easy to make more money but we can never get back our time.

Here's what you'll get out of this book. You'll be set up as a virtual real estate boss. You'll discover how to start doing deals and making money all across the country without even leaving your house if you don't want to. And you'll be able to do as many deals or as little deals as you desire depending on what your income goals are because this is a true lifestyle business.

You can work as much as you want, you can work as little as you want. You can do as many deals as you want or as little deals as you want depending upon what your goals are. You have the power to create the lifestyle you want to live. You don't have to be chained to a nine-to-five job anymore.

You have the choice and the power to design your own life. You need to understand that because it's so powerful. You can work when you want, where you want and how much you want.

All right, so let's talk about what virtual real estate investing is all about. First, I'm going to tell you what it's not. It's not wasting time, it's not driving around for hours to find deals. It's not being a slave to your phone and it's definitely not wasting time, meeting every seller lead you get. You don't have to do that.

Instead, it is about choosing the best markets to invest in, because real estate has market cycles and real estate market cycles are local to specific states, counties, cities, and zip codes. We're going to go through all that and show you how to do that.

Real estate is not a nationwide cycle. Every area in every state has a different real estate cycle, so when your local backyard may be in a hot cycle or a bad cycle, you don't have to invest there. There's plenty of other markets that you can go to that are on an expanding market cycle that are great to invest in at that time.

It's working the market cycles, choosing the best markets that you want to be in and it's getting sellers to call you instead of you chasing deals So, the system that I've designed for marketing brings deals to me. It brings deals to me, so I get to pick and choose which deals I want to work on and it's all about automation. Automating calls and automating making offers because once you implement the same systems and processes I use in my business, it's not difficult.

You don't have to be running around chasing your tail all day doing all this busy work meeting sellers and making offers and all of that. You don't have to be doing all that. It's easily outsourced once you have the system and the right processes in place.

This business is about doing a lot of deals from your home or wherever you may be traveling without meeting buyers and sellers in person. That's old-fashioned techniques and old-fashioned strategies. You do not need to meet in person to do residential real estate deals, you just don't.

You've got to get that into your mindset and change your thought pattern. That is the old-school way of doing things. The new-school way of doing things is virtually on the internet, email, telephone, digital bandit signs, and social media. This is the new smarter way of doing real estate. We're working smarter, not harder!

What I want to do now is I want to show you the evolution of the virtual real estate investor. If you've never done virtual real estate investing before or if you're new to real estate investing altogether, you'll start out as a virtual wholesaler. So, you'll start out doing virtual wholesaling where you can do virtual wholesaling across the country without even leaving your house.

This is the simplest, easiest way to get started as a virtual real estate investor because you don't need any cash to do virtual wholesaling and you don't need to use your credit and you really don't need anything except for your time to set up the relationships with their joint venture partners and then lining up the deals and putting the pieces together, that's all you need. You don't need any cash, you don't need any credit.

Now, once you get good at virtual wholesaling then you will outsource it. You'll have somebody take that over for you where you can move to the next stage. The next stage of the business is going after big profit checks. The big profit checks come with virtual rehabbing. And now virtual rehabbing lies in you being able to rehab properties, fixing and flipping properties without even going to the property.

How cool would it be for you to be able to buy a house for a hundred thousand, put forty thousand into it and then sell for two hundred thousand without even seeing the house? I do it all the time and it's so much fun because if you get involved in the day-to-day minutia of rehabbing houses, you will waste a ton of time, you'll be working on one house at a time and won't be making a lot of money.

Virtual rehabbing is very, very powerful once you get to that stage. And then stage 3 is virtual cash flow investing. Virtual cash flow investing is where you're going into emerging markets that are expanding, rents are going up and where you can still get into multi-family houses and single-family houses to get a cash on cash on return of at least 15% or greater.

This is where you start to build real wealth in your business. Virtual Investing is so powerful because if you live in a market where the house prices are very high, let's say like a hundred or two hundred thousand dollars per unit, you can go to a different market where the prices are lower and the cash flow is greater. Let's say you're trying to buy a four-plex and in your market it's four hundred thousand for a four-plex.

The problem is once the prices get so high for multifamily properties, they don't produce any cash flow, they're really bad investments. We don't want to buy multifamily properties, where the cash on cash return is not 15% or higher. So instead of buying overpriced properties, the solution is virtual cash flow investing, where we can go to these great markets in other states in the Midwest, where the prices are still very low and the rents are high compared to the price that you can pay for the unit.

You're getting great cash on cash return at fifteen percent or greater. So, cash flow investing is great and then after that, you graduate to virtual private lending. With private lending, you actually don't buy properties at all. You lend your money to other investors that are doing all the work for you and you're just letting your money work for you at eight percent or greater interest rate that's a completely passive secure investment for you. That's the Evolution of the virtual real estate investor and that's where we're going.

Now, let's go over the different types of virtual wholesaling and rehabbing. There are two types of virtual wholesaling that I focus on. There's virtual wholesaling to landlords and there's virtual wholesaling to rehabbers. With virtual wholesaling to landlords, you'll be able to sell your properties for a higher price because these are typically properties that don't need as much fix-up and you'll be able to sell them at a smaller discount to the market. Typically, we sell our virtual wholesale deals for more money to landlords than to rehabbers.

The virtual wholesale deals that I sell to rehabbers are typically properties that need a complete renovation which means they need a ton of work. Because of that amount of work that's needed, the rehabbers require to buy them at a much lower price compared to the market value. We'll get into the valuation of the properties and pricing of the properties to your end buyers in the following chapters.

Then there's virtual rehabbing. When you're focusing on virtual rehabbing and reselling, you'll be able to rehab properties in virtual markets or your own market by having a team of people do it for you instead of you managing the process. You absolutely never want to be the one working on a property. That is the worst use of your time that you could ever spend on rehabbing a property.

With virtual rehabbing, you are employing a project manager in the virtual market or if you've developed a strong relationship with somebody that can manage the property for you and bring you deals and/or bring you funding then you'll partner up with that person and you'll share the profits. I've had a lot of success partnering up with people in other markets where they manage the property, they bring the deals and I give them the advice and the guidance and funding for the deal.

Let's talk about keyword research. Keywords are very important for your online marketing efforts because keywords are the words that people search for to find you online. Whether you're looking for people that need to sell their house, whether you're looking for investors that are looking to buy investment properties or whether you're looking for investors that want to lend their money for private lending on your project, it's the keywords and key phrases that will bring those leads to you.

Because keywords are so important, you want to make sure you're using the right keywords so that when they search for you, they can find you. And you'll need to choose the keywords that people use to find you when you are setting up your website and setting up your social media account.

A couple examples to find sellers would be "Sell My House Fast" and with "Sell My House Fast", you would want to use your location. So, if you are looking to buy houses in Cincinnati, you would type in "Sell My House Fast Cincinnati" or "Cincinnati homebuyer" or "sell my house Cincinnati" or "stop foreclosure Cincinnati".

Then you want to use those keywords in your website, in your blog posts, and in your social media profiles so that people are attracted to you, can find you and go to your website, enter their information and then they'll go into your automated follow-up system that you'll have within REIrobot.com.

REIrobot.com already has all of those follow-up systems built in for you and it already has websites that are optimized for these keywords when you tell it which keywords to use. Check out REIRobot.com. You'll be very happy you did. It's a complete All-In-Online Automated Online Investing System

In my online course, The Freedom System, there's a keyword shortcut tool that includes all of the keywords I use in my business. This will give you a shortcut to use the keywords that I use. All you have to do is replace your city and state in the keyword shortcut tool and you can start using those keyword phrases on all of your websites, blog posts, social media profiles, social media posts so people will find you and you'll start generating buyer and seller leads.

Your phone system is very important for your business because it will give you personal time freedom so you don't have to give out your personal cell phone to every prospect or client that you work with. Your phone system will also track where your leads are coming from and that's very important.

If you've never done any lead tracking for your marketing, it's something that you'll want to definitely start practicing and start using because it's like night and day when you start tracking where your leads are coming from especially when you start paying for some of your marketing.

Here are your options when it comes to phone systems. You can either use the free way which is Google Voice. With Google Voice, you get one phone number for free and you get notified of missed calls. The cons of Google Voice is there's no caller ID, there's no call back link and you have to be logged in to make calls from your Google Voice number. There's no call recording which is very important to have.

You're only allowed one Google Voice number so it's very limited when you want to track specific things with your marketing so at a minimum you want a phone number for your sellers, your buyers and your lenders. When you dive deeper, you'll want a separate phone number for your direct mail campaign, for your sellers, for your Facebook campaigns, etc. Those are a couple examples of different things that you want. You want to know where your leads are coming from and what's working what's not working. The only way to do that is to have different phones numbers for your prospects to call.

Alternatively, REIRobot.com has a phone system already built into it and it is the most badass phone system that we have ever seen. Now what it does is basically it tracks all of your marketing. You can set up an unlimited number of phone numbers to track each specific marketing piece.

Each market piece is tracked into its own unique campaign and then it comes up onto a lead dashboard well you'll see how many calls have come in to that number, how many people have sent a text message into that number and how many leads were generated from that campaign. You'll be able to quickly see how much each lead cost and how much money you made from each one of those calls to that specific number. It's really, really, robust and will help you tremendously.

It sends you missed call notifications if you miss a call. It sends text messages and the really cool thing about it is, if somebody calls that number and nobody answers it, it will automatically send them a text message and say "hey I'm busy right now with a client. I'll call you back as soon as I can".

That's very, very important because your prospects are getting an immediate response and it seems like it came from a real person that sent it to them even though it was fully automated. In REIrobot.com, everything is fully automated but with a very personal touch. It appears like its your personal assistance responding for you. It's very smart automation working for you. It has integrated campaign tracking and gives you the tracking numbers as you need them. It has click to text and click to call technology right within REIRobot so you just click a button and automatically call them back. This system is very friendly and easy to use.

Plus, it has all the other features of REIRobot that we don't have time to cover all those right now because the list is endless. REIRobot is a full CRM. It has a full website system, email marketing follow up system, management system, task management and delegation system, and a whole lot more. As they say, the fortune is in the follow-up. REIRobot does the follow for you.

Next, you'll want to set up your social media accounts. Social media sites are places where people go to connect with other investors, get recommendations, share information and promote themselves. People will find you through searching and why you share content. What most people don't know is social media is incredibly powerful for virtual real estate investing. You can build an investor network lightning-fast with social media.

Why do we use social media? We use social media because it helps you look professional. Even if you're just starting out, you can create a presence when you do it right on social media channels. They make you look very professional and you will be very professional after you go through this training and get educated about how to become a virtual real estate investor. You can get a ton of online exposure 100% for free with the strategies that were going to cover.

You can hear about what people think about your business also so that gives you instant feedback, so you can help your business grow and expand. In my online course, The Freedom System, there's a couple of tutorials that walk you step by step how to properly set up your social media profiles in your social media channels.

CHAPTER 3

SETTING UP SOCIAL MEDIA SYSTEMS

Let's talk about how to set up your website. The absolute easiest and fastest way to set up the best website is in REIRobot.com. If you don't already have an reirobot.com account, go set one up. I have many tutorials in there about how to set up your website, you'll want to use the keywords that we just went over in the previous chapter when you setup the name of your website. Your website will be highly optimized for those keywords that people search for.

You can set up 6 different websites in REIRobot and literally all you do is you put in your keyword, you put in your name and hit create, and it creates your entire website for you. It has a full website editor so that you can add pages and remove pages as you need to. It has private landing pages, seller pages, buyer pages and you can customize each website for specific markets, so you can create a different website for each of the markets you're going into.

The websites in REIRobot are SEO optimized, so once you start creating your website, you can add blog posts to it with more keywords in the blog post. This creates more exposure with the search engines. When you have more exposure with the search engines, more people will find you. When you add more blog posts to your website the search engines are going to see that and they're going to like that, and then when people search for those keywords your site will pop up on the top of the search engine rankings.

The prospects your looking for in your target market are going to find your website. They're going to fill out the form on your website and they'll be automatically put into REIRobot's automated follow-up system. It's really, really powerful and I know you'll love It. So, go set that up now at reirobot.com and see the tutorials at reirobot.com for the step by step website set up and let's continue with the next chapter.

CHAPTER 4

FREE WAYS TO FIND SELLERS

This chapter will show you how to find deals and how to find motivated sellers to work with. We do this many different ways. We can find deals from co-wholesaling with joint venture partners, social networking on social media accounts, or by working with realtors in some areas. Some areas are conducive to using Realtors and some areas are not. We find them from REO's.

REO's are bank owned Properties. The exact acronym stands for Real Estate Owned which means Bank Owned. Bank owned properties are properties that the bank has taken back in foreclosure and it is the third step in the foreclosure processes. The first step is when the homeowner goes behind on their mortgage payments. When they go behind on their mortgage payments for three months or more, the lender files foreclosure then it becomes a pre-foreclosure.

The pre-foreclosure process can last for several months up to a couple of years. If the homeowner has not cured the default, the bank will hold a public auction on the Property. You can go there and bid on the property. Sometimes it's in person but most counties do them online now. You can see most of them from Auction.com

The challenge with bidding on auction properties is you need to have immediate cash to close on the property. You need to have cash in 24 hours and those contracts are very difficult to wholesale because they need to be closed within 24 hours. It doesn't give your buyers enough time to do their due diligence.

The 3rd and final stage of foreclosure is if the property doesn't sell at auction. The bank takes it back as a bank owned property otherwise known as REO, Real Estate Owned. REOs can be very, very great deals depending upon the area.

You'll find some markets have more REO's than others and in the areas that have fewer REO's, they're not going to be as great of deals because there's going to be a lot more competition fighting over the deals. Because all REO's are now listed on the MLS, they are some of the easiest properties to find. The easier it is to find a deal, the less of a deal that it's likely to be because there's going to be naturally more competition because its an easier deal to find.

That's why you'll find in some markets on the MLS, there are not many good deals because the MLS properties are the easiest to find properties. This is why finding deals on the MLS depends on the market because each market is in a different stage of hot/sellers' and cold/buyers' market. You'll find more MLS properties can be turned into deals in a colder/buyers' market.

The strategy is to make a lot of low offers and test the flexibility of each seller. You don't need to go see the properties before you make an offer. You need to see if they will negotiate off their price 1st.

My partner and I have a software program that automates all the offers for us. The program sends out hundreds of offers per week so we don't have to do it. We're only interested in the counter offers we get back. If you're interested in using this software in your own business, you can see how it works here:

Automated Deal Maker Software Demo:
www.virtualrealestateinvesting.club/ADM

Another place we find great deals is on Craigslist. Craigslist is also a great way to find buyers as well as sellers. We build our sellers and our buyer's list from posting on Craigslist as well as finding sellers posting properties. Another great way to find deals is by calling For Sale By Owners. We refer to them as FSBOs. You call FSBOs from the for sale by owner sites on the internet. There's alot of FSBOs on Craigslist as well as well as Trulia.com and Zillow.com which we'll get into.

Let's talk about Co-wholesaling. Co-wholesaling is another term for joint venturing with another investor or multiple investors on one deal. It's working with another investor to do joint venture wholesale deals.

The first way is to go through other investors to find deals for your cash buyers. In this situation, I have the cash buyer and I'm going to go work with another investor that has worked and found a deal from a seller. That co-wholesaler brings the deal into the picture and then I take the deal and sell it to my cash buyer. So, we work together to get the deal from the seller to a buyer, we work together and split the wholesale fee.

The other way is to go through investors to find cash buyers. Let's say I'm working in with a seller directly in a particular market and but I don't have a cash buyer or buyer for that property in that market. I can work with other investors in that market and I can bring my deal to them and they can sell it to their buyer and we split the wholesale fee 50-50. So, there are two ways to do it. Either way, works great. I suggest that you focus on building your buyers lists because your buyer's list is an asset that you can use over and over and over again.

Just one person on your buyers list could buy 10, 20, 30, 40 houses from you, so you want to foster and build that relationship with your buyers. Bring value to them by bringing them good deals. You'll become known as the go-to person in your market for being able to get deals sold fast because you've got a hungry buyers list of people that trust you, know you and like you. Developing that buyer's list and giving them value is how you do that.

Then there's networking. Networking is a great way to get deals. You want to look for sellers who want to sell quickly and let everyone know that you are. That's a potential source of deals so tell everybody that you're looking for houses where a seller wants or needs to sell quickly. Get the word out. Tell people what you do. Describe the seller situations that you're looking for.

You are looking for people that are motivated to sell quickly. Maybe they're falling behind on their property taxes or their mortgage payments? Maybe they got divorced or lost their job? These are all potential situations where you can come in and help them.

Are they in a situation where the household income has gone down from either a job loss or a divorce or something like that? If so, they may not be able to keep up with their bills or their mortgage. If they've fallen behind, they're going to need to sell the house and you can help them liquidate that property fast.

You're a solution provider for them. Typical situations are foreclosures, behind a payments, inherited a house from a relative that passed away or they're going through a divorce or some other hardship. Other real estate investors are the best people to network with because they know people and other investors. They can introduce you to other investors. They have a buyers list and an investor list. They also probably have a private lender list if they've been in the business for any length of time.

Local Investors know which title companies to use in that virtual market. Network with them and just make friends. That's it... Just make friends with people. That's what networking is about. You don't have to go to that virtual market to do your networking in person because you can do it all on social media and it's really easy.

You don't have to leave your computer or your house to be able to network with people. Network with anyone that can refer leads to you consistently. These also include attorneys, accountants, CPAs, and mailmen. Why mailman? Because they know which houses become vacant first!

Social networking is one of my favorite way to find deals. Social networking is like networking on steroids. You're able to find active investors through Facebook groups, LinkedIn groups, YouTube videos, and Instagram. It's very, very powerful. I suggest you start with Facebook groups because it's the easiest.

I have some social media tutorials in my online home study course, The Freedom System. If you own the Freedom System, make sure to watch those tutorials and then set a plan to actively networking on these platforms on a daily basis. It will only take you 20 minutes per day. You want to create a habit of doing that every day. That habit and that activity of networking with people on social networks will flourish into a big network of people you can do business with. Continue building and develop that habit by continuing to do that on a day to day basis and you will be rewarded for it. I promise you.

There are also realtors. Real estate is their job. Some people have a negative connotation of Realtors. Some people have a positive connotation of Realtors. I would advise you to make friends with Realtors. Make friends with them because they can help you find deals and make offers. They can help you sell properties. They can help you pull comps and give you pocket listings. Pocket listings are properties that are not even on the MLS yet and some of them are REO agents.

When you tap into an Realtor that's an REO agent listing properties for the banks, you've hit a gold mine because you're able to get that inventory from them early before anybody knows about it. You can find the REO Agents from the Auction websites because their REO inventor will be listed as auctions on these sites: Auction.com, Hubzu.com, Xome.com and other local auction sites. Develop relationships with those listing agents even if their current listing isn't a property that you're interested in.

Develop a relationship with them because if they're actively listing property, they're going to be listing more properties and they may come across great deals that need work or the seller wants to sell it as-is. You can take that deal and you can turn that into a great property for your business because a lot of sellers don't want to do the work and they don't want to list it with an agent. Agents prefer to sell houses that are beautiful because it's much easier for them.

In order for an agent to sell that house quickly, you're the solution for them so make friends with agents. You can have agents set up searches for you that email you when new properties are listed that match your criteria. This is a great way to develop a relationship with them even though you may not need it. Maybe they can show you some properties that you're not seeing.

You can also setup searches in Realtor.com, trulia.com, and Zillow. Each site has a section in the search criteria for keywords. You can type in these keywords individually or all together and it will spit out properties that meet these criteria. These results are going to be your potential deals.

Short Sale, Bank Owned, REO, Estate Sale, Handyman Special, Needs Work, TLC, Motivated Seller, SOLD AS IS, Probate, Motivated, Fixer, Must Sell, TLC, Cash,

Quick Close, Needs Updates, Needs Updating, Trust, Trustee, Auction, Foreclosure, Make Offer, Any Offer, Homepath, Homesteps, Fannie Mae, Seller Financing, Bring All Offers

So, these are also the keywords that you want to give your agent(s) that are going to find properties for you. They just set up searches for you one time, it's going to continue to email you new properties as they're listed to your email. You can use those properties for practice. Take them from your email, print them out or look at them online and evaluate them.

You got to start practicing so you can learn how to find the good deals from the bad deals. REIrobot has a built-in deal analyzer. You can take those deals and put them into the deal analyzer. REIRobot's deal analyzer has a red light green light system to tell you if it's a good deal or a bad deal and these are great properties to practice on.

Give these keywords to your real estate agent. Tell them you're looking for properties that have these keywords in the description. They'll be happy to set it up for you because it's a potential commission for them. You want to work with the agents that are actively listing properties because these are the agents that are going to be able to bring you pocket listings.

You can find these listing agents that are listing these types of properties by searching for properties yourself in sites like trulia.com, Realtor.com, Zillow.com. Go to these sites and select the area you want to buy and try some of these keywords. You'll be able to see the listing agent contact information. Call them, email them, text them. Tell them what type of properties your looking for and develop a relationship with them.

EXAMPLE OF WHAT TO SAY TO THEM:

"Hi My name is _____. I'm a real estate investor and I'm looking for properties that need work that I can buy below market value. If you happen to get any new listings, I'd appreciate it if you showed it to me first and I'll give you an instant offer the same day of any property that you bring to me that you haven't listed yet. "

They will bring you properties believe me.

And then there's REO's. REO's are vacant bank owned homes. The owner fell behind on the mortgage and they lost it. The bank took it back in foreclosure and now it's a bank-owned home listed for sale with an agent or on an auction site.

You can find REOs on the major auction sites.

Hudhomestore.com
Hubzu.com
Auction.com
Xome.com

Go to these sites set up a free account. After you set up your free account, you can go in and create a search criteria. Select the state, the city, and the zip code you want to buy properties in. Set the price range your desire and then the sites will send you email alerts when a new property matches your criteria. These sites are great because they give you 30 days or more to close on the property which means you have time you time to contract it and sell it if you want to wholesale it and you have time to line up funding if you want to buy it and Rehab it.

These sites are great to find properties to wholesale, rehab or buy and hold. When you get these email alerts, start evaluating these deals. It's great practice even f you don't bid on them.

Craigslist is another great source of leads. You can create posts on craigslist for free. I post one ad every day in each market. Post them in the services, real estate and housing categories.

Let talk about For Sale by Owners (FSBOs). You can find FSBOs from searching property listing sites on the Internet. Make a list of the properties you find that meet your criteria. Start calling them and making offers on the properties. Make notes on your conversions. Follow up with them every 30 days because they will become more motivated over time as the house hasn't sold or what they are asking. They will become more motivated to take your offer or negotiate with you.

There's a shortcut for this in REIRobot com called a Lead Swiper Campaign. The Lead Swiper campaign automatically drives motivated seller leads from Craigslist into the REIRobot dashboard. It automatically creates the list for you of For Sale by Owner homes. It captures all the contact information and it puts it all nice and organized in the lead dashboard within your REIRobot account. It's really sweet.

So, here are the other websites that you can visit to find FSBOs. zillow.com has a search criteria you can select for FSBOs. Trulia.com also has a FSBO search criteria. You'll be able to find the FSBO checkbox criteria on these sites in the FILTERS section.

Craigslist is a common place for homeowners to post their home for sale by owner. Those are all great sites to find for sale by owners.

You want to make a habit of doing that on a regular basis and make that part of your success plan to go to these sites, find these properties, make a list, call them, follow up with them and get their information and make them an offer

Making offers is how you make money in real estate. You've got to get out there and get started doing this stuff. I'm giving you the step-by-step process of how to do it. We're starting with finding deals first and then we're going to move through the rest of the steps in the buying and selling process.

Set an initial goal to call 100 FSBOs. Make a list of 100 of properties that you like that you think would be good deals and call them to get the seller form filled out.

Up till this point, all the strategies we've discussed have been free strategies. We're going to switch gears a little bit. I'm going to discuss a couple different ways to find sellers using paid advertising. If you're just starting out, you probably don't want to use these right away especially if you don't have the marketing budget to do it. If you do have a marketing budget and want to generate a high number of leads quickly, this is what you need to do.

Paid advertising is the easiest way get more leads and deals quickly. When you do paid advertising, sellers start calling you more than you call them. This is because you're paying to put your marketing out there and they are responding to it and asking you for an offer on their house.

Direct Mail is very effective because you can get very specific lists of properties to send small mailing to. It's very expensive to send a postcard or letter to everyone in a zip code. What if you could send to only the most motivated prospects in that zip code. This is the benefit of direct mail. You can select specific lists of properties that are highly likely to be very motivated to call you when they get your letter.

One of these specific lists is the Vacant Property list. This is the list the post office has identified as vacant homes. How do they know? Because they deliver the mail. When the mail doesn't get picked up anymore, they know the house is vacant and they stop the mail service. This vacant house list is available in REIRobot as an upgrade.

You can also advertise on Google, Youtube and Facebook via pay-per-click campaigns. For example, when people go to google and they search for "sell my house fast", you can set your ad to show up on the search results pages. Then they can visit your website and request an offer on their house or call you. On Youtube, you can create a video ad and show it to people looking to sell their house. On Facebook, you can use an image or video ad and show it to older people that don't need their house anymore.

And then there are bandit signs. Bandit signs are the little cheap signs you see by the side of the road normally near red lights and intersections where people can see them when they stop. You can use bandit signs in a lot of different markets and depending upon how hot the market is will determine how effective the banner sign is. You can either put these out yourself or get somebody else to do this for you which is more efficient.

CHAPTER 5

TAKING CALLS FROM SELLERS AND CALLING SELLERS

Making offers to sellers is how to convert leads into deals. Making offers is a very fun part of the business. Sometimes, you'll make offers directly to sellers and sometimes you'll need to go through an agent if it's a listed property. When working with listed properties, you'll make your offer to agent and the agent will present it to the seller.

When working on FSBO property, you talk directly to the seller which is great because you can better negotiate your terms when there is no middleman. Call them, interview them to uncover their motivation and you find out what their situation is. They will tell you why they're selling. This will help you when it comes to structuring your offer.

Don't be afraid to call sellers. They want to sell their home because they listed it for sale. They want you to call them. Call them and practice. Ask the questions on the information sheet. Get the information sheet filled and out tell them you'll get back to them because you need to do some research on the property. After you research the comparable sales and run the numbers to establish your offer price, call them back and make an offer.

Who cares if they don't accept your Offer? At this point, you just need to practice get out there. It doesn't matter if you screw it up. There are tons of houses in the world of people that people need to sell. Just get out there and practice. You're not going to get any results until you start practicing.

SELLER INFORMATION SHEET

Can I get your name? _____

Property Address: _____

City: _____ Zip Code: _____

Cell Phone: _____

Email Address: _____

How did you hear about us? _____

Can you tell me a little about the house? (like how many bedrooms/bathrooms/sqft?)

____ BR ____ BA ____ Car Garage _____ Sqft

Does it need any repairs? _____ No _____ Yes

(If yes) A lot or a little? _____

Is the house listed with a Realtor? _____ No _____ Yes

What have you done to try and sell it? _____

When do you want to close? _____

Why are you selling it, anyway? _____

Is the house free and clear, or do you have mortgages on it? _____

How much do you own on the mortgages? _____

How much are you trying to walk away with? _____

Do you need all of that now or can you take payments for some of it? _____

OK, we are going to do some research on the property and see if the property qualifies.

Will you be ready to get the paperwork done if the property meets our criteria? _____

When is generally the best time for us to reach you by phone?

GREAT, I'll be back in touch with you shortly to let you know if the property qualifies. Thank you and have a great day!

All right and the next section we're going to cover is if you are working in a local market in your backyard, if you choose to work in your local market and you think it's a good market to start in then do it then, do it. I'm not saying that you can't work in your local market but virtual investing is not just about investing in other markets that are in other states or in other areas, it's a system of outsourcing and getting people to do the work for you as well as working in virtual markets that could be in a better marketer or an easier market in another area. So, if you can work in your local market, great do it as well as some other virtual markets outside of your area.

CHAPTER 6

WHAT'S IT WORTH?

In this chapter, you'll discover how to find the after-repaired value (ARV) of your subject property. The ARV is the value the property will be worth after its fixed up. Before you can make an offer on a property, you need to research the property and find out the after repair value. We do this by looking at the comparable sales which are what other nearby homes in similar condition have sold for recently.

You can find sold property data from Zillow.com or TotalViewRealEstate.com Be careful Not to use the Zillow Zestimate because this is not an accurate reflection of what the house is worth. It does not take into account the condition of the property and repairs needed to make it "Like-New." You can use the individual data for each property from Zillow because this is simply a reflection of public records of what the properties sold for.

We need to use like-kind properties that have recently sold in the neighborhood around your property that you are considering purchasing. The closer to your home the better. If it's in the same neighborhood, that's better. If you have to go outside of your subdivision, try and stay within a quarter of a mile. If there are still none in the quarter of a mile then go to half a mile. If it's a more rural area and there are not many comps within the half a Mile, then you can go out to a mile.

You want to find at least three comparable homes that have sold within the last three to six months. If you can't find any within the last three to six months, you can go to 12 months. It's better if you stay close to your home then there are two variables for finding more properties if you can't find them within half a mile, within three to six months, it's better for you to stay close to your home and go out longer like a year instead of expanding the radius around your property.

It's better just to stay close and go out longer because when you go out further away from your home, neighborhoods can change very, very fast. The neighborhood a mile or two miles away may be very different than the neighborhood that your subject property is in. You want to stay close to your subject property as possible. The same subdivision is the best. Half a mile radius is the standard. If you can't stay in the same subdivision, then go out a half mile.

Then you want to look for the houses with a similar amount of square footage. You want to use a 20% variance when you're looking for other homes that have sold. For example, if your house is 1000 square feet you want to use comparable sales that are anywhere from 800 to 1200 square feet. That's the 20% variance range. You just take your square footage and multiply it by 0.2 and subtract it by either square footage. You take your square footage and multiply it by 0.8 to get the low amount and then take your square footage of your subject property and multiply it by 1.2 to get your high range. All of the comparable sales need to fall in between the high and low range of your square footage.

For our example a thousand square feet you're looking for something 800 to 1,200 square feet and those that are the range of the home that you'll use for a comparable sale. You also want to look at the number of bedrooms and number of baths. You want to look for houses that have a similar or close to the number of bedrooms and Bathrooms your subject property has. So, it is a 3 Bed, 2 Bath house, you want to look at 3 Bed, 2 Bath Comps. This is the accurate way to find comparable sales.

And then you look for a house that is already sold. This is very important. They must be sold comps. Houses that are listed FOR SALE, are not valid comps. Here's why. I might look at the same house that was listed for 300,000 but then it ended up selling for $220,000. Well, that $300,000 value is not real. The $220,000 value is real because it was sold. Somebody bought it for $220,000. Nobody bought it for the $300,000 because it was probably overpriced and we don't want to use overpriced for sale properties as our comps because that will cause us to pay too much for the property.

If you don't want to do all your comparable manually by hand, you can use REIRobot to do all of it for you because it has a built-in property analyzer that gives you the value with 1 click. It does all of the variance calculations. It finds all the comps around your property for you on a map and you just pick which ones you want and then it takes those comps and puts them into the formula that I'm going to show you in a second and it automatically gives you the after repair value, it's really slick. REIRobot does all that for you. You don't need to go to Zillow if you're using REIRobot.

Here's how you calculate the value after you've found the three properties that you'll use. These should be the three on the higher side because you want them to be the value of the property after its fixed up.

Take the top three light kind comparable sales and calculate the Price Per Square Foot by dividing the sold price by the square footage. Add the 3 price per square foot together and divide by 3 to get the average price per square foot.

Example:

Sold Price	Square Footage	Price Per Square Foot
$167,000	1100 sqft	$151/SQFT
$175,000	982 sqft	$178/SQFT
$195,000	1132 sqft	$172/SQFT

$501/3 = $167 Average Price Per Square Foot

Then you multiple the $167/sqft average by the square footage of our subject property.

$167 x 1000 = $167,000

Our After Repaired value of our example subject property is $167,000. That's what you'll use for your after repaired value. This is the manual process that I just showed you but if you're using REIRobot just go to "run the comp model" and it will analyze the deal and give you the value automatically.

CHAPTER 7

MAKING OFFERS

In this chapter, you'll discover how to make offers to sellers and I'm going to give you several proven formulas to use. When you follow these formulas, you should have no trouble finding a buyer for your deals. These formulas set the prices properly for deals you're looking to sell. If you buy it yourself to rehab it, or if you'll or to use it as a rental property then you'll know that you're buying it at the right price.

Before you start, you need to always find out what the maximum offer price is. For wholesaling to a rehabber, your maximum offer price will be 75% of the ARV minus the repair costs. For wholesaling to a landlord, your maximum offer price should be 85% of the ARV minus the repair costs.

Let's see what that looks like. Here's the first example that we're using, now this is wholesaling to a rehabber. Your max offer price will be 75% of the ARV minus repairs. We're going to use our example number that we figured out for an ARV which is $179,000. Multiply that by 0.75 and you've got $134,250.

$$\begin{array}{r} \$179{,}000 \\ \underline{\times\ .75} \\ \$134{,}250 \end{array}$$

That adds in a 25% profit margin for the rehabber which is very good. Then, subtract the repairs needed of $23,000

$$\begin{array}{r} 134{,}250 \\ \underline{-\ \$23{,}000} \\ \$111{,}250 \end{array}$$

If you we're buying this property to rehab it yourself, $111,250 could be your maximum offer price. However, in this situation you're not going to buy yourself, you'll wholesale it to the rehabber who's going to buy it for that price. they're going to take it, put the $23,000 into it and resell for $179,000 or more.

In this situation, you need to build in your profit as the wholesaler. The way we do that is we just subtract our profit. For this deal, lets set your profit at $10,000. Subtract $10,000 for your estimated profit to get your maximum offer price.

$$\begin{array}{r} \$111,250 \\ \underline{-\$10,000} \\ \$101,250 \end{array}$$

$101,250 is your maximum offer price in order to wholesale it to a rehabber and make approximately $10,000 profit as your wholesale fee. That's what you'll offer the seller to wholesale for cash to a Rehabber.

Your Offer to Seller: $101,250

Your Price to Sell it to a Rehabber: $111,250

Now, let's look at a different scenario. Let's say the property doesn't need as much work and it's in a rental neighborhood. You can flip this thing to a landlord buyer that wants to keep it as a rental.

You'll wholesale it to a landlord. Your maximum offer price will be 85% of the ARV minus the repairs. Take that same $179,000 ARV, multiply it by 0.85 and that leaves you with $152,000.

$$\begin{array}{r} \$179,000 \\ \underline{\times\ 0.85} \\ \$152,150 \end{array}$$

Subtract the amount it would cost to repair this property as rent ready which is $13,000

$$\begin{array}{r} \$152,150 \\ \underline{-\ \$13,000} \\ \$139,150 \end{array}$$

You could always buy it at that price, put it in the $13,000 and rent it out yourself it for the long-term hold. In this situation, we're going to wholesale it to a landlord and we're going to take out our profit.

Let's set our wholesale profit in this scenario for $20,000 and subtract it.

$$\begin{array}{r} \$139,150 \\ \underline{-\ \$20,000} \\ \$119,150 \end{array}$$

$119,150 is our maximum offer price to the seller. We're able to pay a little bit more for this property in this scenario because it needs less repairs and we're also building in ourselves double the amount of profit because we can sell it for more money.

Every deal is different. This is why it's important to get mentoring when you're starting a new business especially real estate. The deals are so profitable, its very expensive when you lose out on a deal. Just 1 deal could pay for your entire mentorship program.

To see if mentoring is a good fit for you, apply for free session at
www.virtualRealEstateInvesting.club/Apply

Can you see how powerful it is to be wholesaling to landlords instead of wholesaling to Rehabbers? It can double your profit when you find the right deals and flip them to landlords instead of wholesalers.

Those are the two examples of how to structure offers. Scenario 1 was a wholesale to rehabber deal. Scenario 2 was a wholesale to landlord deal.

Now, let's throw a twist into the mix. Now, what if your offer price is too low for the seller and they come back to you and say "oh no I can't take that because I owe more than what you're offering."

Your Response should be: "Mr. seller, how much do you owe?"

Seller responds back and says: $129,000

Your Response should be: "Well Mr. Seller. I still might be able to help you. Would you be willing to sell the property for what you owe on it?"

Seller: Yes, I just want to get out from under it.

You've just negotiated yourself a free house by simply asking 1 question. This is the same way I bought the house my family and I live in. This is called buying the house subject-to the existing mortgage. There's no money to give the seller. There's no money needed to buy the house because mortgage stay's in the seller's name. You simply take over payments on their mortgage.

You can easily sell the house on Lease Option or Owner Financing. You collect a Non-Refundable Option Payment from your lease option buyer and collect monthly rent. You make the monthly mortgage payment from the rental income and the leftover positive cash flow is yours to keep.

These Lease Option Buyers don't care the houses isn't in perfect condition because you're giving them an opportunity to buy their own home when they can't go to an agent. They can't go to a realtor and they can't go to a bank because they can't get a bank loan because their credit is less than perfect. This is the only way they can buy their own home and you are providing that opportunity for them.

Lease option buyers are more than happy to give you $5,000 down or $10,000 or $15,000 down on the house and then pay you a monthly fee to buy the house.

Normally the monthly payment will be several hundred dollars more than the underlying mortgage payment. This is positive cash flow from a free house! Plus, you got the five to fifteen thousand dollars up front that's a non-refundable deposit.

This is a creative strategy to work with sellers that owe more than your cash offer price. It's a very, very effective strategy to use to create incredible positive cash flow without using your own cash or credit.

CHAPTER 8

OVERCOMING THE TOP 5 OBJECTIONS

You've made your offer to the Seller. Now, what? Are they going to say "yes"? Are they going to say "no"? If they say yes, then you've got yourself a deal. If they say no, then it's most likely one of these five objections of why they said no. A "no" does not mean its not a deal. It means we need to keep going with the process.

The deal is not dead yet just because they have an objection. We can overcome that objection with them. In this chapter, we'll cover how to overcome the top five objections you'll hear from sellers when they say no.

The number one objection is the offer is too low. This is the most common objection that you'll get. Some sellers are just not realistic. They want to hit the lottery with their property, or they want retail price even though the property needs $40,000 in repairs. This is what I mean by not realistic.

Your job is to show them the realistic picture of what they're going to get for the property. Typically, their only other option is to list it with an agent. We need to show them what they're going to get when they fix their house up, list it with an agent and wait for a buyer to come and buy the property. The way that we do that is with proof on paper. We do this by showing them a "the seller net Sheet."

The seller net sheet shows them that our offer is better than what they're going to get when they fix up their house, list it with an agent, wait and keep paying their monthly fees and mortgage, and all their monthly expenses on their home. Show them that you can close quickly, and they don't need to do any of the fix-up, and they're going to get more than if they fixed it up themselves and listed it with an agent and waited for a buyer. If you're active member of the Virtual Real

Estate Investing Club, you can login to the members area and download a copy of my Seller Net Sheet.

Print this worksheet out and fill it out for the particular property you made an offer on. Send it to the seller and then call them and go over it with them over the phone. This is what they would get if they fix their house up and listed it with an agent. Sellers are focused on the prices homes are listed for around the neighborhood and they don't realize all the costs involved.

This shows them reality of what they will walk away with after doing all the work, investing money in their home and waiting to sell. It really brings it home that your offer is a better deal. With your deal, they don't have to wait, they don't have to keep paying their mortgage, they can move now.

Remember the seller questionnaire you filled out when you had the 1st call with the seller? This is the time to make sure you are solving their biggest pains and motivation of why they need to sell their house. If they need to sell fast and they need to move, then this is your chance to give them that.

Give them the offer they need so that they can get more than what they would get if they fixed their house up and waited six months for a buyer. In most cases, they can't wait, or they don't have the money to fix up the house. So as long as you give them more than what they would net on the sheet, then your offer is a no-brainer for them. You can do for them what a real estate agent cannot do. Be confident that you have the solution for your seller.

The number two objection is I'd rather fix it myself. You'll do the same thing you did in number one but make sure you have the repair cost in there. Tell them to go get some bids from contractors. Give them the scope of work. Actually, write up the scope of work for them or have them write it up. The scope of work includes everything that needs to be done to the property to sell for the full retail value (ARV). Give them some names of retail contractors. These should be the most expensive contractors in your town, like the people that have the largest Ads in the Yellow Pages.

These are the types of contractors these sellers would be calling because this homeowner doesn't want to do anything in the construction process like managing subcontractors so a retail contractor will come in and they're going to do everything for the homeowner. The homeowner doesn't need to be involved in anything and they're just going to write them checks, big checks.

You want to get a couple estimates from those people and have the seller do it so that they choose the process and do the process, work with the contractor to do that and what are you going to find is the costs are going to be way higher than what you predicted for them. And also tell them that its not the end of the end of the story because usually it's going to cost a lot more and take a lot longer than what the contractor tells them because of the add-ons.

They're going to find more things that need to be fixed, and then the homeowner may request other things to be done during the process, and those are all add-ons. The add-ons typically add another 20% to the costs.

The number three objection is "a realtor told me I could get more" How many times will you hear that? Well, the first thing you need to do is go back to the seller net sheet again, show them what they're going to get at the end of the day from the agent. This is the real number the agent is not showing them.

The agent is telling them, "I can sell your house for 300,000, I have buyers that are interested in this house. I'll bring them over next week." It's BS, they don't have anybody. All they're going to do is put the property in the MLS and wait for a buyer to come and look for the property. Most agents don't really do much at all except for a list the property in the MLS. There are exceptions of course.

Ask them: Is the agent's price guaranteed? If they can't find a buyer, are they going to pay you that price for the property? No, no they're not. Let them know your price is guaranteed. Your offer is guaranteed. Do they have the time to let the property sit on the market and let an agent list it and wait for a buyer?

No, they want to sell it now. You can buy from them now. You just need to talk it through with the seller and overcome these objections. Do they have the money to make the repairs?

The agent will require them to make the repairs before they list the property. Do they have the money and the time to do that? No they don't and the agent is not going to pay for the repairs needed for the property either. This is how you easily overcome "a realtor told me I could get me more."

The number 4 objection is "my house doesn't need much work. The new homeowner can do it." Show the seller pictures of recently sold homes in the neighborhood. Show them these houses were in pristine condition and let them know their home in its current condition is not going to sell for the same price unless its fixed up to look pristine like the others. Ask them questions: "Do you think your house is in the same condition as these?" "Which house do you think a buyer would choose if they were priced the same, this one or yours?" These questions will help the seller draw their own conclusions without you forcing it on them.

They need to come to the realization themselves that they are dreaming that their price is too high considering what the condition of their property is. Point out the obvious to them. I've seen it hundreds of times. Most sellers downplay the amount of work that's needed in their home. Make them understand how much work is needed.

New homeowners just want to move into a house. They don't want to do anything to the property. They don't want to do anything. They just want to move in and be comfortable and enjoy their new home. They don't want to come in and start doing all of this work to a property.

The last objection is "I'm just going to rent it out." Well, the first thing the seller needs to consider is, will the house generate enough rent to cover the mortgage, the taxes, the insurance and the maintenance?

Most often, sellers that have never rented out properties don't figure in all the costs involved after they move out and someone else moves in. Educate them a little bit on how expensive that can be and how they can get upside down very quickly especially if the house is vacant because a tenant moved out and left it a mess.

They need to consider the maintenance costs. They need to consider putting away ten to twenty percent of the monthly rent into an escrow account for repairs and maintenance. Most new landlords never account for the repairs and maintenance. They take their rent money and pay the mortgage, taxes and Insurance and then there's nothing left over.

What happens when one of their rental properties needs repairs, they have no money to make those repairs and then the tenant leaves because the property isn't being maintained. Now they have an empty house and the empty house is not being rented which means they're not getting any rental income. Because they don't have any rental income, they can't pay the mortgage or the taxes or the insurance. This turns into a very motivated seller because they can't pay the mortgage, it goes into foreclosure, they ruin their credit just because they thought, "I'm just going to rent it out." Now they're in an even worse situation.

You need to paint that picture to them.

You need to ask them "Is this really the best decision for your future" Think about the long-term play here, do you want to risk ruining your credit because not being able to maintain the property, not having enough cash flow in the property and having a tenant leave and you're not able to rent it out because your property's not in livable shape anymore?

Make them realize that being a landlord is a whole different ball game than being a homeowner. Can they afford the maintenance on the house, can they afford to pay the mortgage during vacancies, can they afford to fix up the house when there's nobody living there? They'll need to have reserve funds available to be able to cover the mortgage and be able to fix up the property in between tenants. do they have that? If the answer is no, then it's not the right time for them to be a landlord. Do they owe any back payments to the lender? Because if they owe any back payments to the lender, they need to make those up before they can put a tenant into the property.

Those are the top five objections. That's how to overcome them with your sellers and I guarantee you when you convey the rebuttals to these objections in a clear and concise way, they will understand.

You'll get them just to see reality of the real situation that they're just not seeing right now. That's your job when you get a "no." Don't just raise your price. That's not going to work because that's going to turn into a bad deal for you. You need to stick to your offer. You may be able to come up a little bit but that's going to cut into your profit. The better way is to overcome their objections and get them to see the reality of the situation.

CHAPTER 9

GETTING THE CONTRACT SIGNED

Congratulations! You've got the seller to say "yes" to your offer. Now, the question is "how do you get them to sign the contract"? Because you're here and they're in a virtual market, you can't meet, you don't want to, how do you get the contract sign?

You've got a couple different options to get the contract signed. You could email them the contract, they print it out and sign it. To get I back to you electronically, they can scan it and email it, fax it to you, or take pictures of each page with their phone and text it back to you. Anyway, that works is fine!

You could set up set up a DocuSign account where they can digitally sign the contract from their computer or phone. However, you don't need to because there's an alternative to DocuSign that's free because it's included in REIRobot. REIRobot does this for you but it does even more. REIRobot has a built-in document generator. All you need to do is click a few buttons and REIrobot will fill out your paperwork for you for each seller and buyer. How cool is that?

REIRobot will send the contract to them by email and they click a few buttons to digitally sign it and it will be emailed right back to you. There's nothing for the seller to print, scan or fax and you've just secured yourself another deal. Now you can move that property to the selling phase and go and sell that property to a buyer. That's it, that's how you get the contract signed.

Another option is to hire someone to go out and meet with them. Mobile notaries do this all the time and they are not very expensive. They bring the document for the seller to sign, put it in front of them, they sign it, and the notary takes it back and emails it back to you. You can find a mobile notary at 123notary.com. It's a very simple way to do it and it only cost you a few bucks.

CHAPTER 10

PROTECTING YOUR CONTRACT

All right, now we're talking about protecting the contract or otherwise known as protecting your paycheck. I would love to be able to trust 100% of the people I work with all the time, but sometimes we need an insurance policy to make sure that we keep the people honest that we're working with and this is how we do it. There are two different ways to do it depending upon who you're working with. If you're working with a wholesaler or an investor that's bringing you the deal, you need to have them sign a non-circumvent agreement. There's a non-circumvent agreement in the Freedom System you can download and use for your deals.

The non-circumvent agreement protects you. It means they can't go around you and go directly to your buyer and cut you out of the deal. This protects your paycheck and this is a legal document that you can show to the title company that's closing the deal to make sure that you get your assignment fee and you get paid your piece of the profit from the deal.

Make sure whenever you're working with an investor that you sign a non-circumvent agreement before you ever introduce them to one of your buyers. When you co-wholesale or joint venture with an investor, they bring in the deal to you and you bring the buyer or vice versa. In this situation, you need to make sure you have a non-circumvent agreement signed with that other investor before you ever show them your buyer or seller.

Before you even send that property out to your list, you want to make sure that you have this document signed. That's going to protect you, to make sure the investor doesn't go directly to your buyers' list and cut you out of the deal. So that's how to protect yourself when working with an Investor.

Now, let's discuss how to protect yourself when working with a direct seller. I'd love to be able to trust every seller that I work with too, but we need an insurance policy to keep them honest as well and this is how you do it. When you're working with a seller, when you present your offer and get them to sign the purchase and sale agreement, you'll include one more document to the end of that purchase document.

This is called the notice of purchase and sale agreement. This document is very, very effective. When they sign the Purchase and sale agreement, you'll have them sign the notice of purchase and sale agreement as well and then after they sign it, you'll take it to a notart where you will sign it in front of the notary. The notary will notarize your signature and then you will record this document on public records.

It only cost $10 to record this document and it's going to protect you so that when other investors go to that seller and offer them more than you offered, this document is going to protect you. It prevents the seller from taking a higher offer from someone else.

If they accept that offer and they try and close on that property, the title company will not close on that property because you will be in control that property by having this notice of personal sale agreement signed and recorded. They already signed a legally binding contract with you. If they go and sign another contract with somebody else, they are violating that contract. They're breaching that contract which is illegal.

This notice of purchase and sale agreement keeps them honest to make sure that they can't go and sign another purchase and sale agreement with somebody else. They won't be able to close on the property with that other buyer. When you have the Notice of Purchase and Sale Agreement recorded, you control the property. You have the right to buy that property.

Sometimes I elect not to buy the property. Why would I do that? Because if the seller really wants to work with this other buyer and they're getting more money from this other buyer, then I will agree to let the seller sell the property to that other buyer however, I need to get paid to release the Notice of Purchase and Sale Agreement from the property.

Whatever my assignment fee was going to be to sell that property for the seller, I'm going to request that amount of money from their transaction. This is called the release of lien. By having this Notice of Purchase and Sale Agreement recorded on the property, it's a lien on the property. It clouds the title. The title company or the closing attorney will not close the deal with this record against property.

So, I will agree to release my lien from the property when I am paid from the title company. This is all handled by the title company so you can be sure you get your fee when you sign the release and the title company gets the lien released so they can close the deal. That's how you make money from this type of transaction when you are giving up your right to sell the property. That's how you protect yourself. This is the end of this chapter and I'll see you on the next.

CHAPTER 11

FREE WAYS TO FIND BUYERS

Let's talk about the best free ways to find buyers and build your buyers list. I'm going to cover several ways to find buyers and build your buyers list.

Real Estate Investment Associations (REIA) are great to attend. They usually have monthly meetings, and this is where you can go and network with new and seasoned real estate investors. You can find great vendors for your business and find properties for sale and find buyers looking to buy properties. You'll also meet local private lenders and hard money lenders. I highly suggest you attend as many REIA's as you can.

Network with everyone can. Take as many flyers as you can find. When you get home, go to all the websites on the flyers and join as many lists as you can especially if they are from wholesalers because they'll start sending you deals.

This is how networking works. You want to join buyers lists so you can get deals from them. Evaluate every deal that comes your way and see if it would be a good to sell to your buyers list. Then you could work on a joint venture deal with them. To do a joint venture, you either add your profit to their price or you talk to them and ask them if they will split their profit with you. There are two ways to do it and its very easy to do.

Facebook groups are a great way to network with people and build your buyers lists. Here's the best way to do it. Login to your Facebook account and Join Groups related to real estate in the city you're targeting.

Let's say for example, you're targeting Cincinnati. Go into Facebook groups and you will type in "real estate Cincinnati." The search results will show you all of the groups that are in Cincinnati relating to real estate. Join all of those groups and start interacting with people.

The best way to interact with them is to send direct messages to each member of the group separately. You want to do this privately in Facebook messenger, not in the group feed where everyone can see. I suggest you contact 10 people per day. Just simply start a conversation with them, tell them what type of deals your looking for and ask them what they are looking for.

Get their email address and phone number so you can add them to your buyers. I manage my buyers list in REIRobot because it keeps it all organized for you and whenever I get a new property, I simply click a few buttons in REIrobot and the property gets sent out to my entire buyers list via email and text message. It's an incredibly powerful platform.

Meetup.com is another great way to find investors to network with. You can get deals and sell deals to many people you'll meet on meetup.com. Go to meetup.com either on your computer or on your phone and search for real estate group in that city. Type real estate + the city that you're working.

For Example, search for real estate Cincinnati and you'll find all of the meetup groups there. Join the groups and a lot of times you'll be able to get email addresses of the members of that group and you can contact them by email to start networking with them so you can add them to your buyers list and you can get on their buyers lists.

Google search results is a great way to find other wholesalers to buy from and sell to. Simply go to google.com and search for "sell my home fast (city)" Of course replace (city) with the city you're targeting. For example, search for "Sell My House Hast Cincinatti" and click search.

What you'll see is all the homebuyers that are paying for ads for people searching for selling their house in Cincinnati. You want to visit every website on the page and sign up for their buyers list on their website. Sometimes it will be called "VIP Investor List" or "Wholesale Properties" or "Investment Properties." You get the idea.

You also want to email them and call them and introduce yourself so you can find out how to send them wholesale deals. These guys are paying money to get found on google. I guarantee they will buy your deals if they're priced properly. These are typically bigger buyers and they will buy every good deal they find.

Craigslist Ads are also a great way to build your buyers list because people will respond to your ad for a property for sale because they're looking for wholesale deals and then you can automatically add them to your list through your website. REIRobot has a website builder that makes it very easy to setup your own website. You can have a website up and running in 10 minutes.

Anywhere you go you should be networking with people. Tell people what you do. Realtors are also a great source to network with.

Don't overlook those "we buy houses signs." Whenever you see a "we buy houses" sign, I want you to call the number on the sign. Whenever I see a "we buy houses" sign, I call the number, introduce myself, tell them what I'm doing, tell them what I'm looking for, ask them to add me to their buyers' list. I also get their information to add them to my buyers' list. This is the mindset you need to get into.

Everything we're doing here is building your network. You want to continue to focus on things that build your network. You want to join buyers lists and you want people to join your buyers list. When you go to REIA's, trade business cards with people. Get their business card, give them your business card. If you don't have a business card or if they don't have a business card then get their information. Get their cell phone and get their email address and their website if they have one.

Look for other wholesalers that are selling properties. Sometimes you can bring fliers instead of a business card. You can hand out fliers to people so just print it out from your computer. Alot of times at real estate investment meetings, they have a section where they allow people to stand up and say a few words about what their haves are and what their wants are. Get up there and tell people what you're looking for and what you have to offer.

Local Facebook groups are awesome. I love local Facebook groups. Search for local Facebook groups on Facebook either on your computer or on your phone. Here are some keywords to search for:

real estate investing + [City Name]

real estate investors + [City Name]

real estate + [City Name]

That's how you find the local Facebook groups. Make sure you include the city or the state or the county.

Look for the investor groups on Facebook and join them. You can also look for agents and just other general real estate groups as well.

Meetup groups are also very effective for virtual networking, what most people don't know is that meetup groups are very effective online. The purpose of meetup groups is to have a local physical meeting but I use them a little bit differently. I don't go to the local meetup groups but I do find the local meetup groups online for any virtual market that I'm targeting. Alot of times there's an email list within the group, sometimes it's public sometimes it's private.

I focus on the public meetups where you can find the email list and you can send an email to the whole list of that meetup group or you can copy and paste the email addresses and send them out individually or add them to your buyers list in REIRobot. You want to join as many meetup group as possible because it's going to expand your network very fast. Not many people even know about this, never mind doing this.

Start conversations with people in these meetup groups and you'll be able to find a lot of buyers and a lot of deals quickly.

Always be networking. Tell everyone you know what you do. Tell them that you're looking to buy houses and tell them that you have wholesale houses and fixer-uppers for sale. Either they're going to be interested in buying a house or selling a house or they might know somebody that has a house for sale.

Whenever you're out there networking, it's always an opportunity for you to get the word out about your business. Think of where you might meet a bunch of investors and go there, so that's why we like to go to local real estate investing Association and Club meetings because that's where they congregate. Think about the places where they congregate online.

Search for those places online where they congregate like the meetup groups and Facebook groups and LinkedIn groups. Join as many online groups as you can start talking to people. It's the cheapest way to grow your business. Think about those places and maybe you can find some new sources on your own. Virtual networking from your phone or from your computer is very, very effective. If you don't have time or don't want to do it yourself, you can have a Virtual Assistant do it for you like I do.

In this business, you got to work with what you got. So, what does that mean? You have to work with the resources that you have to work with. You either have more money than time or you have more time than money.

You need to determine which one you are, to determine how you are going to market for your sellers and market for your buyers. If you have more time than money then you'll use the free ways to find buyers and sellers. If you have more money than time, then you should be looking at the paid ways to find sellers and buyers.

I'm going to go over the paid ways to find buyers, this will be an abbreviated version because I want to make you aware of where you could go when you get to the point where you have more money than time. One of the ways that we use is direct mail to landlords to build our buyers list.

We send direct mail to landlords just like we talked about in the zip code matrix. You use that actual list that we created in that search criteria in the list source example.

The key is to select absentee owners that have paid cash for a property. The mailing address is different than the subject address that means they own the property as a landlord. They have a tenant in the property and they purchased it within the last six months and they're the same zip codes that you're targeting. The zip codes that you've identified to target are the zip codes you want to pull this list from and the similar properties that you're targeting.

You can target those investors that own properties with a similar square footage range of the typical rental property that you're targeting. This will give you an exact match of the buyers that you want to sell your new properties that you're getting to and because they've bought in the last six Months, they're very likely to want to buy another one. So you pull this list and you send them a direct mail piece to them and you want to send this to them frequently, so it's not just one-off postcard you send to them one time, you want to send a series of them like five to seven postcards.

Because most people respond after you've touched them five to seven times, you'll get the best response rate from your campaign after you send 5-7 mail pieces to your list. Sending one postcard is not going to give you much of a response. Sending five to seven will. You want to space those out every 30 to 45 days so you stay in front of them and as they're looking for new properties you can be on their radar and then they can contact you and you can add them to your buyers list. Every postcard should be a little bit different to appeal to them in a different way.

You can also send postcards to cash buyers. Send a postcard campaign to the cash buyers list out of reiroboot.com. You could export it and do a direct mail campaign that's managed through REIRobot and then you can also do Facebook ads.

Facebook ads are a great way to find buyers for your properties. With Facebook ads, you can select the zip code that you want to target and you use a house for sale as the ad. You'll either use a real property that you have for sale or a ghost ad. A real property you have for sale is preferred. But if you don't have one yet, you can use a type of property you intend to sell. This is what a ghost ad is.

This does two things, you're finding a buyer for that house and you're also building your buyers list as well. That buyers list is an asset that you're building. You will invest a little bit of money into the Facebook ads and into the direct mail campaigns which is building an asset, your buyers list, you can continue to use over and over again for free. You pay for it once to get that list and build that relationship with that buyer's list and you can continue to use it over and over again. It's very, very effective.

CHAPTER 12

QUALIFYING BUYERS

You're going to come across a lot of people that present themselves as buyers. Sometimes some of them are just co-wholesalers that are going to take your deals and try and sell them to another buyer. What we're discovering in this process is how to pre-screen buyers and qualify them to be real buyers that can close on the property themselves.

About 10% of the investors you come in contact with and add to your buyers list are going to be real buyers. This 10% is what you want to focus on because they're going to be able to buy multiple properties from you all the time and you'll be making a lot of money through these relationships. It is very, very,

very productive for you to spend time and identify the people who are going to be your real buyers.

When you get in contact with a potential buyer, you want to pre-qualify them as quickly as you can using the buyer questionnaire. If you have the Freedom System, you can get the Buyer Questionnaire from Module 4.

Based on the type of deal they're looking for, they will fall into one of five categories. They're going to be either a rehabber or a landlord willing to do some repairs, a turnkey landlord that doesn't want to do any repairs or a combination of those or they're going to be a wholesaler that's just looking to either wholesale the property. Those are the types of buyers that you're going to be in coming in contact with and the seller questionnaire is going to help you identify which one they are.

You want to try and determine their experience level. You want to find out if they're new, experienced or if they're an expert buyer. You also want to find out what cities and neighborhood they're most interested in. This is going to help you to sell your properties faster because when you get a property prospect in that neighborhood sometimes you can go and contact your real buyers and say "hey I got this deal over here would you be interested in this neighborhood, would you be interested in this price point"

If you've got a potential deal from a seller, you're just not sure if it's a deal or not, sometimes you can lean on your real buyers to give you some interest before you actually lock it up under contract. You need to be careful about it so that they don't go around you and go directly to the seller. Ask them what their buying criteria is. (i.e.: how cheap do they need to buy. how much profit do they need to make in the deal?)

Make sure to always capture their name, phone number and their email address so that you can contact them when you find a Property that meets their criteria. The cell phone number is most important to get from them and email address because you'll enter them into your REIrobot database to be included in your email and SMS blasts when you get a new property.

Find out how they fund their deals. This is the most important question that you need to ask so make sure you don't forget to ask this question: "How are you planning on funding deals that I bring you?" and just be silent and listen to what they say.

Funding options range from cash, line of credit, private lender, hard money lender, and traditional bank financing. That will determine what deals you can bring to them because if they're funding the deals with cash you can bring them any deal in any condition.

If they're funding it with the line of credit, that's very similar to cash because they have full control over the money. They can use it for whatever they want. They can use a line of credit as cash and buy any deal through that.

If they're funding it with a private lender, the private lender may want to approve of the deal. This one might be a little bit more difficult to get financed than cash because they might want to see pictures of the house, a repair estimate, comps or an after repaired value appraisal.

A hard money lender is going to be a little bit more strict than a private lender because they're going to have certain guidelines of how much they can lend on the property. They also may require the buyer to have some skin in the game. Hard money lenders also lend the money for repairs but they're going to keep that money in escrow.

They'll release the money to the rehabber as the repairs are done. The property can be in any condition because hard money lenders lend on properties in all conditions.

Traditional financing is one that you get from your bank or from mortgage broker. Typically, traditional financing banks and lenders are going to want to see the property in good shape. They're going to want to see the property in good shape.

If it's in really bad shape and the buyer wants to keep the property, they'll either need to buy with cash, fix it up with private funds and then refinance it with a traditional financing bank after it is nice and pretty and in good shape. Banks don't want to lend properties on properties that are not livable. It needs to be livable in order for a traditional bank to finance the deal.

This is how you prequalify and pre-screen your buyers so you can find real buyers.

CHAPTER 13

MY SHORTCUT TO RAISING MONEY FOR DEALS

This is a quick, yet very powerful secret I've discovered to add to the buyer questionnaire that I want to share with you. This secret can lead you to a lot of cheap private money you can use to do a lot of deals with. This is the easiest way to raise money for your deals.

What you're going to do in the buyer questionnaire is ask cash buyers this question to find out if they're interested in joint venturing with you. The first thing you want to do is get their attention and this is what you'd say:

"Let me ask you a question... what if I told you my company can handle the entire deal for you even after you buy it."

They'll say something like:

"oh well I might be interested in that" or they say "no I'm not interested. I already have a team"

This is your response:

"so basically, here's how it works. I find the deal. I fix it up and sell it. All you have to do is fund the deal and we split the profits at the end of the deal. As you know finding deals is one of the toughest pieces of the puzzle in today's market. Managing the rehab is just a pain in the ass and I'm doing all that for you. This is why we have many crews in place to handle the rehabs for you and we have proven systems to get the house sold at the end of the deal. Does that sound like something you'd consider?"

Then just be silent you wait for the answer. They'll say yes if it sounds good to them or no or maybe and maybe is an opportunity for you to continue the conversation with them.

This is very powerful strategy I discovered that can convert investors into private lenders by using this scripting. This format captures their attention and solves the big problem that they have because they don't really like to manage rehabs, they just do it because it's good money so if you can do that for them and they can do more of them by letting their money work for them then they're going to be happy because they're doing less work and they're making more money in the long run.

Use this strategy. It will be very effective and you'll be able to raise a lot of money with the cash buyers that you talk to.

Chapter 14

SETTING THE PRICE OF YOUR DEAL

We've already discussed how to set the offer price for the property and now we're going to discuss how to set the price to sell the home. It really depends on how how much in repairs the property needs. So if you're selling it to a rehabber then you'll sell it for 75% of the ARV value minus the repairs. Just make sure you have enough profit for your wholesale fee built in.

Of course, you can try and sell it for more if you are in a hot market where there aren't many deals. You can always lower your price or accept a lower offer.

It's much easier to lower your price than to increase your price. Here's our example:

$179,000 ARV
X .75
$134,250
- $23,000 Repairs
$111,250 Min Selling Price

To sell it to a Landlord, you'll sell it for 85 to 95 percent of the ARV minus the repairs.

$179,000 ARV
X .85
$152,150
- $10,000 Repairs
$142,150 Min Selling Price

If you're selling it as a turnkey property to a landlord, then you'll sell it for full retail price. So those are basically the very simple mathematics of how to price the property when you're selling it to a rehabber, when you're selling it to a Landlord, when you're selling it to a turnkey landlord.

CHAPTER 15

METHODS OF CLOSING DEALS

There are three different ways to close a deal. This depends on how you acquire the deal. There are a couple other factors that we need to discuss.

The first option to close the deal which is the easiest and simplest way is to assign the property to your buyer. This will make sure that you get paid the profit that you need to wholesale the deal as well as keep the transaction in one single transaction. It's the simplest and the easiest way to close the deal. You get paid an assignment fee from that transaction.

You should use an assignment agreement when your profit is $10,000 or less. When your assignment fee is $10,000 or more, you should use a double-closing. The benefits of using a double closing are that you don't have to show your profit to the buyer.

Typically, when you're working with an end buyer, a cash buyer or landlord buyer, they don't mind if you make a fee because you're adding value. You're doing a service for them, you're bringing the deal to them and you are facilitating the transaction for them which has value. They don't mind if your profit is typically $10,000 or less. When your profit gets to be over $10,000, they start to get a little squealing because they think you're making too much money.

The way to protect yourself from this is by doing a double-closing. A double closing is basically two different back to back transactions on the same day. You have a transaction with your seller to buy the property and then you have a transaction with your buyer to buy the property from you.

It happens on the same day and the funds from your buyer close this deal and then you use those funds to give to the seller and you collect the difference. This is the reason why you don't need to use any of your own cash or credit to do these types of deals. The Funding is provided by the buyer who you are selling the property to.

There are more fees involved with the double closing, however, if it's a really good deal and your profit is $10,000 or more, it's worth it to protect yourself.

Sometimes you'll need to use transactional funding for transactions where it's not allowed for the buyer to fund both transactions during a double closing. This will all depend on where the deal is and how you acquired the deal and what the title company allows. The best way to get around this is to use a different title company.

Make sure when you are buying properties from banks or online auction sites you use your own title company. Do not use the banks title company. This is your right as the buyer to choose to use your own title company. The bank's title company is too difficult to work with and will always require you to use transactional funding which will cut into your profits and add extra hassle for the deal.

An assignment agreement, you sign a purchase and sale agreement with the seller to buy it for a certain price and then you sign an assignment contract with the buyer who pays an assignment fee and shows up at the closing as the buyer. The best way to do this when you're doing an assignment type transaction is to have a contract with the seller and another contract with the buyer to sell the property. At the closing, have them sign the assignment agreement because that's going to disclose your profit and if everybody's already there at the closing table ready to do the transaction, they're not going to complain about your assignment fee.

You will use the assignment fee agreement to actually close the transaction. However, you're going have that agreement to sell the property to your end buyer just in case you need to do a double closing. With a double closing, it's the same way. You have a contract with the seller. You have a contract with the buyer but it's two separate transactions.

Transactional funding is used with a double closing. The contracts are the same as the double closing. You'll have a contract with the Seller and a contract with the buyer. The transactional funder comes in to fund the purchase for you for less than 24 hours. When you sell the property, the transactional funder gets their money back (plus their fee), you collect the difference.

Those are the three ways to close the property depending upon what type of seller you're working with and what state you're in and whether they allow double closings or assignment contracts or if they require transactional funding.

Most of the time you can't find an investor friendly title company everywhere to do a double closing or an assignment contract. You need to network with local investors to find out who the investor friendly title companies are. Most traditional title companies that work with real estate agents will say they don't do double closings but there are investor friendly title companies that will do them. You just need to find the right title company to work with.

CHAPTER 16

FINDING A GOOD CLOSING AGENT

Let's talk about how to find an investor-friendly title company. This is what you need to look for, you'll need to close your deal in a title company or with an attorney. Depending upon which state that you're working in will determine if you'll be working with a title company or a closing attorney. When possible, I always like to use a title company and you need to choose one that is familiar with creative investing like wholesaling, assignments, double closings and buying houses subject to the existing loans.

You need to find an investor- friendly title company that will do these types of transactions for you. They also need to be able to do title searches quickly for you because in this business you need to move quickly when you find a good deal.

You've got to move fast, take action and put it under contract. You need to get the title search done to make sure that you'll actually close on the property. You also want to work with a title company that is friendly to the way that you do your virtual business so, you need to make sure that they don't require you to show up in person to do the closing and that is very, very common.

A lot of times title companies do not require you to show up in person, they can either email you the documents to sign or they can send a mobile notary to have you sign the documents that need to be notarized. The notary will let you sign and notarize your signatures and take them with them and send them back to the title company for you. That's very easy to do.

Here's how you find an investor friendly title company. Check with the local real estate investment groups. You can find them online and on Facebook and meetup.com. Many times, the best investor friendly title companies will be vendors of the investment club and will be listed right on the website which makes its very easy to contact them.

Find other investors in the Facebook and LinkedIn groups and ask them which title investor friendly title company they like to use. Ask other wholesalers in the area who they recommend. Facebook groups are very effective for this as well. That's how you dig down and find an investor-friendly title company in virtual markets.

CHAPTER 17

MANAGING THE DEAL THROUGH CLOSING

Alright you got yourself a buyer and you've got the deal under contract to sell your deal. Now it's time to manage the process to make sure that you get paid. Here's how to do it. Step number one is you want to make sure that you get your contract signed with the seller and send it to your title company so that they can start the title search.

Number two, you're going to market the house for sale. Once you have the agreement signed with the buyer, send it to the title company so that they can start setting up the transaction. If the buyer is getting a loan, you need to call them once a week to follow up to make sure that they're on track with their loan.

Make sure you have the contact information for their mortgage broker so you know their mortgage broker is on task and got all their documents and has the loan submitted for approval. Make sure that the appraisal is ordered from the mortgage broker so that that doesn't hold up the deal.

Keep in communication with the seller the whole time to maintain that positive relationship. When the title company is ready to close, they're going to send you the settlement statement otherwise known as the HUD statement for you to review. This to make sure that everything looks good and most importantly your profit in the deal looks good.

The last step is printing and signing the closing paperwork and overnighting it back to the title company so that you can get paid. Make sure to sign the papers with a notary for any documents that need to be notarized. That's how you manage the deal through the process.

CHAPTER 18

MAKE MORE MONEY PER DEAL

The first stage of the automating your businesses is learning how to make more money per deal. In this step, you'll learn how to work smarter, not harder. This relies on you learning how to be a better negotiator through experience. When you learn how to make better offers on your properties and how to estimate repairs more accurately, you'll be able to make better offers.

You can also go back and renegotiate with the sellers to get a better deal as well. So that determines that comes from your inspection. Once one of your buyers go out to see the property, you'll get feedback on what needs to be done to the property.

By looking at the pictures from the people that you send out to go inspect the property from WeGoLook, and by having your buyers go see the property, you'll get feedback on the repairs of the property. The repair list and that scope of work will increase which will give you the opportunity to go back to the seller and renegotiate the deal and get a better deal for yourself which you'll be able to make more profit in the deal.

You'll be able to spot better opportunities because you're learning. Your knowledge base is increasing and the more you learn, the more you earn. As your knowledge base is increasing, you're learning how to take more deals and more leads and turn them into deals. You'll be able to do more deals by taking more leads and structuring them more effectively into deals. That will allow you to make more money per deal.

You'll discover how to maximize profits with multiple exit strategies. The more exit strategies you have the higher conversion rate of the leads will turn into deals. You'll be able to figure out how to take those deals where the seller owes as much as the property is worth and wholesale those deals as subject to deals. You will be able to create multiple profit centers for yourself throughout your deals. Multiple exit strategies include wholesaling, retailing, wholetaling, owner financing, lease options and buy and hold. These strategies are going to be very, very critical for you to maximize your profits as you grow your business.

Wholesaling itself has multiple exit strategies. You'll be able to wholesale to rehabbers, wholesale to landlords, and then wholesale to turnkey landlords. Retailing is where you'll be able to go through and virtual rehab properties.

Virtual rehabbing involves you finding a good project manager to manage your rehabs or when you start working with people in those markets, you'll find by developing relationships with people.

You'll find people that you talk to comfortably that you trust and are adding value to you, you're adding value to them. These naturally evolved into virtual partnerships where you'll be able to take those partnerships and those relationships and convert them into a virtual rehab partner.

They will manage the virtual rehab deals in those markets for you. Before you know it, you'll have virtual rehabbing partners up in multiple markets! When you get into virtual rehabbing, you're able to turn your profits from that $5,000 -$10,000 profit into $40,000 - $50,000 profits by not wholesaling the deal, funding the deal with virtual funding partners and then rehabbing the property and retailing the property to a homeowner.

That's where the big profits start to come in. Just take it one step at a time. You will get there but you need to start developing these relationships first, start practicing deal negotiation by doing wholesaling and then you can evolve into virtual rehabbing.

Sometimes, you'll find great deals and you'll be able to wholesale properties to end buyers where the homeowner will buy the property from you in as-is condition. This is called wholetaling. You won't need to rehab it at all and instead of selling it to a landlord, you can sell it to an end buyer. They retail buyer will come in with a new loan and finance the property so it's going to be a 30-day closing and you'll make bigger profit spreads of $20,000 -$30,000 without even having to touch the property.

These are typically properties that you find that won't need much work. They're just going to need cosmetic work and you'll be able to sell them for retail price or near retail place like 95% of retail price and the homeowners willing to do the work on these properties because it's a great neighborhood that you found the deal in and it's a desirable school district and they just want to live there. They're ready to buy the property and they'll buy it in as-is condition because they want to live in that location.

When you find these clusters zones of these neighborhoods that have great school districts and the inventory is very limited, you will find retail buyers that are willing to buy the property and fix it up themselves and these are gold mines. This is something that you'll focus on to increase your profits by 200-300% on these deals.

There's also subject-to deals. Subject-to deals are great deals to hold onto for yourself and this will give you multiple profit strategies in these deals. Buying a house subject-to means you are taking a property over from a homeowner. You're taking over their payments on their existing loan so you don't need to get a new loan to buy the house.

This is a great strategy because you don't have to raise money for these deals because the funding is already in place on the deal. You're just taking over the payments on their loan then you turn around and sell the property on a Rent-To-Own or Lease Option. I love selling on lease option!

With lease option buyers, you don't have to deal with the issues that you typically have to deal with when you're renting a home. You don't have to do the maintenance on the property buyer it's the lease option buyers responsibly.

They will also improve the property for you. It's amazing what they will do to improve a home they don't own. They'll do stuff like cosmetic repairs and add decks to the back of the house because it's their home. They want to make it comfortable for them to live in. They will actually increase the value of the property for you.

There are three profit centers when you do a subject-to lease option deal. You'll get a non-refundable option deposit when you sell them the house, then you'll get a monthly spread on the rent. You'll get cash flow every month of the difference between what they pay you for rent and what you're paying on the underlying mortgage from the previous homeowner. Then when your lease option buyer refinances the property in two to three years, you'll get a big profit check from all the equity that has built up in the house. BOOM!

Sometimes they just move out of the house and you get the house back and you can do it all over again. This is the 4th BONUS profit center! I call these yo-yo houses.

There's also subject to seller financing and there's subject to wholesaling. You can also buy a house subject to from a homeowner and then sell it on owner financing. In some areas like Texas where they don't like lease options, you can sell it on owner financing.

You can also do subject-to deals where you don't keep the house yourself. You get a home subject to the existing mortgage from the seller and then you wholesale it to somebody where you're just collecting a wholesale fee and you're taking that deal and giving them ownership with the deal immediately. For those types of deals, you can make $10,000 - $20,000 right up front by wholesaling that subject-to deal. The profit comes from you finding that great deal with the underlining financing already in place. This will come from your marketing efforts. Subject-to deals are great virtual deals to do.

After you have more cash flow in your business than you need, you can start to buy and hold the best properties that come your way. This is what I call virtual cash flow investing. You'll come across these properties that are two units, three units, four-unit houses and in the right neighborhoods. In the right virtual markets, these are great cash flow properties to hold on to for long-term wealth building.

Another way to make more money on wholesale and retail deals is negotiating better prices and finding buyers who will pay you more. Who are those buyers? Typically, they are landlord investors. When you only sell to rehabbers, you limit your profits because they're very savvy buyers. Landlords are going to pay you more for the property because the properties don't need as much work.

You'll also increase your profits by getting repairs done faster. When you're rehabbing, you are testing out different contractors and different construction crews. You'll find the better construction crews that you'll hold on to. When you do that, your costs are going to go way down which will increase your profits because you'll be able to get your repairs done faster which means you'll be able to sell that house faster which means you'll pay less in interest payments on the loans that you're getting to borrow to fund those houses and repairs.

Another great strategy to increase your profits is the offer partial financing. When you're retailing houses and your end buyer doesn't have enough money for a down payment, you can offer to take a second mortgage on the house and help them out with their financing.

You could either give them 10%-20% second mortgage so they can get into the house with a smaller down payment. You'll get monthly payments on that second mortgage which will allow you to sell the house for a higher price. You'll also be getting a monthly cash flow stream for 10 -15 fifteen years which will greatly increase your monthly positive cash flow for every deal you do.

You'll come across homes that are free and clear which means they don't have a mortgage on them. These are great houses to structure seller financing on with the homeowners because you can structure great financing that you don't need to go borrow money to buy the house. The financing is built into the property and you can structure many times 0% financing because you're just there asking for a particular price on the property.

Let's say you find a property where the seller is asking $100,000. Instead of trying to negotiate the price down as low as you can go, instead you offer to pay the full price the seller is asking. In exchange for you giving them their full price, you'll get good terms and those good terms is spreading out that $100,000 price over the course of 15 years of monthly payments.

That's a great way to buy houses because you can turn around, you can sell those houses on lease option, or on owner financing or you can keep them as rentals. They will have great cash flow because of the monthly payments for seller finance free and clear homes are very, very low. Buying free and clear homes and selling on lease option can be the perfect marriage.

A lot of times lease option buyers can't get a loan. That's why they're buying the house on a lease option. They can't qualify for a mortgage with a bank or a lender. They'll give you a large deposit just for the right to be able to buy their own home plus pay more than the market rental rate which increases your cash flow.

You'll want to start marketing for Lease option buyers when you're using this strategy. Its very easy to find them. Selling on lease option is the easiest way to sell a house.

You pre-qualifying them based upon how much they can afford to pay for your down payment and how much they can afford to pay for your monthly payment. You want to look for those buyers that have larger down payments. That's going to increase your profit margin and your cash flow immediately by getting a larger non-refundable option payment.

I've had people give me non-refundable option payments for $50,000 and $80,000 dollars to buy my houses on lease option. This is a very, very effective strategy to get a lot of your profit out of the house upfront and then you get the rest of the profit at the end when they refinance the home.

You can also sell lease option homes for higher than retail value. Typically, I sell a lease option for 110% of the current value of the property because we're selling it at a future value. We're selling it at next year's price and you can also build into your contract that the price that they pay will increase three percent or five percent or ten percent a year until they close on the property.

There are going to buy the property at the market value when they close on the property. You are getting to enjoy the appreciation and the tax benefits of the home while you still own it and you can also rent them out. The rent payment on a lease option is higher than a normal rent payment because they are buying the home.

CHAPTER 19

HOW TO DO MORE DEALS

We are talking about how to do more deals to make more money. You do more deals is by getting more leads of deals. What you need to do is generate more leads. We do this by doing better marketing. We're doing better marketing by hiring virtual assistants to do the free marketing for us and then you can scale that as much as you want. You can hire as many virtual assistants as you want to replicate all of those three ways of doing marketing. And then also adding in paid marketing to really skyrocket the amount of lead flow that you're getting into your business.

The operations of your business need to match the lead flow. If you're getting too many leads in and you don't have enough people to call those leads, that's going to be ineffective for you. You need to make sure that you have your virtual assistants set up that are going to talk to all the leads that you're generating for your business.

Once you get this really nailed and figured out, your business will skyrocket. You'll dominate the markets that you're in because then you can focus on the truly motivated sellers in those markets. Because you've got so many leads coming in you can cherry-pick which ones you want to work with which will produce more profits for you.

You always need to track your marketing. When you start doing all of this marketing through the free ways through your virtual assistants and through the paid ways, you need to track your marketing so you know where the leads and deals are coming from. REIrobot does a fantastic job of tracking your marketing. There are many ways the campaigns in REIrobot track your leads. It can track them through, email addresses, phone numbers, webforms, lead swipers via craigslist and whole lot more.

You will know what your exact return on investment is of your marketing dollars for each specific marketing campaign you do when you look inside of the lead campaign dashboard within

REIrobot. You'll be able see what parts of your marketing is working and what is not working so you can turn off what's not working and do more of what is working.

An important part of scaling your marketing is split testing. When you learn how to split test different things, you'll be able to optimize your campaigns. You'll learn what produces more leads and what doesn't produce the deals. The end result is you want to focus on the deals closed. I don't really care how many phone calls I get from a postcard campaign.

I care how many deals are generated from that, how much profit comes from that because the end-all goal is to give you a return on your marketing dollars, not to get the phone to ring. If the phone's ringing and you're not able to do any deals from those calls, then you're wasting your money.

You want to focus on the return on investment. When you look inside the campaign dashboard in REIrobot, it gives you that return on investment which is how much you spent on the postcard campaign and how much money you made from that campaign. When you learn how to test different postcards and different messages using different lists, you can compare all of those results to find the highest return on investment for your marketing dollars.

Craigslist Ads are very easy to split test because they're free. You can post as craigslist ads as you want. Have your virtual assistants post as many craigslist ads per day as you want in all different markets to get the phone ring which will get the leads pumping into your websites. Any kind of advertising you do, you should be split testing your marketing to optimize the results.

You want to be investing in the most effective marketing methods. That means you'll apply to the 80/20 rule. Focus on the 20% of the things that you do that are bringing the most amount of money and stop doing the things that you're doing that are not bringing the most amount of money. Don't let fear hold you back. This is a step by step process. You're learning how to do it yourself and then you're outsourcing it and automating it so that you can have true freedom in your business.

You'll soon be the business owner that just manages your business from your dashboards in REIrobot and you'll have a truly virtual business where you can be at home or anywhere in the world managing your business.

CHAPTER 20

AUTOMATING YOUR BUSINESS

Let's about automating your business. This is the engine that runs your business to give you true time freedom in your life. There are three things that you want to automate in your business. You'll want to be doing these things yourself first so you can understand and become an expert in these things before you decide to outsource them.

Your marketing is number one. Your lead intake is number 2 which is taking calls from buyers and sellers. You want to be doing that yourself so you can get comfortable talking to sellers and buyers. Number three is the sales process. The sales process of disposing of your deals should be the first thing you outsource.

So let's talk about automating your marketing. Marketing is the number one thing you need to get all organized yourself. If you have the Freedom System, use the action plans as your guide to get your marketing organized. The reason why I did the action plans for you was so that you could get organized.

It allows you to set a 90-day goal and then chunk that down into a weekly goal and then chunk that down into a daily goal. You're going to delegate those goals to the virtual assistants you hire to do your marketing for you.

You have been tracking what has been working and what marketing activities have been bringing in leads. You were testing those things yourself, so you want to give your virtual assistants the things that we're working for you so they can automate all those activities for you. Then they can continue to do those for you, automate those things for you and then scale them up. You can hire different virtual assistants to do different marketing tasks in different virtual markets for you.

Utilize the technology that we built for you. REIrobot was built for our personal business and we saw the need for so many people use it for their own business. We set it up into a system where you can use it as well. Over a million dollars has been invested into that platform for your benefit. So use the technology that's already there for you.

It automates a lot of things in the business and it's a platform where you can manage your team through. You'll know exactly what they're doing on a daily basis and the results that they're driving for your business. Virtual Assistants are your friends. Learn to hire and work with virtual assistants because they can literally set you free.

Let talk about automating your lead intake. At first, you're going to have your phone numbers directed to your cell phone. You want to have your seller questionnaire with you for sellers. Bring your buyer questionnaires around for you and have those ready for you. You never know when a seller is going to call. You need to have these questionnaires with you so you can ask the right questions and get their information. If you don't take the call, they might call the next investor and you'd lose out on the deal.

When you get those calls, this is your practicing time. When it's time to hand that over to somebody else, you're going to forward the calls to your Virtual Assistant to do this for you. This is the same with taking calls from buyers. All contacts and properties should be managed in REIrobot. This is your CRM where you can login and see what's happening in your business at all times. You can see what all your team members are doing.

CONCLUSION

Congratulations! You finished the book. I'm so excited for you. If you own The Freedom System or if you're in the VIP Club, you can download the action plans for each step of the business. Make sure to complete every step of each action plan.

In this book, we discussed how get deals, how to sell deals, how to close and everything in between. This is great overview of the Virtual Real Estate Investing Business. If you'd like to go further, I suggest you get a copy of my Freedom System or Join the VIP Club to get the video tutorials and trainings.

You need to organize your marketing calendar because, in order to grow your business, you need to do consistent marketing. That's what it comes down to. Once you've mastered each part of the business, you should outsource and automate each part to virtual assistants. This will set you a free and allow you to be the business owner that manages the business instead of the technician doing all the work in the business.

Take the profits that you've made from the deals that you've done and set them aside for marketing. Set aside profits from each deal to build your team of virtual assistants that can do the free marketing tactics for you and set it aside to start doing some paid marketing methods.

You'll need at least one virtual assistant to help you so get started start finding an interviewing virtual assistant to work with. You'll be very happy you did. The way you become more productive is by having implementers to help you implement things for you.

Remember, time is your most valuable asset. You can never get your time back. You can always make more money but you can never to get your time back. Let people help you. It's very smart to put a team together that can help you. What you're actually doing is you're buying your time back at a discount by using virtual assistants.

This is extremely effective for productivity because you can use your time to do other things. If you want to focus on bigger deals, you focus on the bigger deals. You focus on getting apartment buildings while your team is continuing to do your residential house business for you.

All right, let's get started, I'm so excited for you! Start growing your business and I will talk to you soon. Let's continue this conversation in the VREIC VIP Club. If you're not a member, you can request a membership from my fanatical support team at support@virtualrealestateinvesting.club

Keep Fighting for Freedom,
DC Fawcett

I Will Always Fight For Your Freedom

FREE BONUSES

FREE Online Mini-Course
virtualrealestateinvesting.club/bonus

FREE One on One Strategy Session:
VirtualRealEstateInvesting.club/Apply

Made in the USA
Coppell, TX
14 February 2020